The sociological approach

CW00496098

What is sociology?

The origins of sociology go back to the nineteenth century when it emerged as an academic subject in the wake of the Industrial Revolution that first took place in Britain (1740–1850) and the democratic revolutions of the USA (1776) and France (1789).

1 Offer a brief definition of sociology. `1 mark`

....

....

2 What is meant by society? `2 marks`

....

....

3 Who are commonly regarded as the three 'founders' of sociology? `3 marks`

a

....

b

....

c

....

4 What is meant by the term 'social stratification'? `2 marks`

....

....

5 Who used the term 'sociological imagination' and what does it briefly mean? `3 marks`

The term sociological imagination was used by

....

and means

....

....

....

6 Define the terms '(social) structure' and 'agency'. `4 marks`

....

....

....

....

Classical ideas of Durkheim, Marx and Weber

Emile Durkheim

Emile Durkheim (1858–1917) is regarded as the first academic sociologist who developed a key understanding of the role that consensus values play in reinforcing social order and stability in society. He is also associated with the key concepts of the division of labour and the collective conscience.

1 Which sociological perspective is Durkheim described as laying the foundations for? `1 mark`

....

....

2 What did Durkheim mean by anomie? `2 marks`

....

....

3 Suggest *two* social problems that can derive from anomie. `2 marks`

a
....

b
....

4 What kind of approach was Durkheim trying to show in his study of suicide? `3 marks`

....

....

....

5 Why did Durkheim see the division of labour as becoming increasingly important? `4 marks`

....

....

....

....

....

....

Karl Marx

Karl Marx (1818–83), as a revolutionary socialist, saw modernisation as an opportunity for creating a progressive society that could reflect the interests of the people. The end of history, he argued, will be a truly equal communist society.

1 What did Marx call the economic system he lived in and observed? `1 mark`

....

2 According to Marx, what determines a person's class in this economic system? `1 mark`

....

3 What is the name of the dominant class and the subordinate class in this economic system? `2 marks`

....

....

4 According to Marx, what is the most important driver of social change? `1 mark`

....

....

5 What term did Marx give to the process whereby the subordinate class are duped and fooled into supporting the society that is actually exploiting them? `2 marks`

....

....

6 What does the term 'ideology' mean? `3 marks`

....

....

....

7 What is the relationship between the division of labour and the means of production in capitalism? `4 marks`

....

....

....

....

....

Max Weber

Max Weber (1864–1920) was the most negative of the three 'founders' of sociology, fearing that the emerging industrial society was becoming increasingly bureaucratic and stifling. He referred to the growth of bureaucratic structures as like an 'iron cage' around society.

1 What did Weber mean by authority? `1 mark`

....

....

2 What did Weber mean by charismatic authority? `1 mark`

....

....

3 What did Weber mean by rationalisation? `2 marks`

....

....

....

4 What is meant by the objective approach advocated by Weber? `2 marks`

....

....

....

5 What did Weber believe was the main driver of social change? `3 marks`

....

....

....

....

6 How did Weber see Protestantism as a key factor in the development of capitalism? `4 marks`

....

....

....

....

....

Sociological perspectives
Functionalism

Functionalism originated in the USA in the mid-twentieth century. It is a structural-consensus theory centred on how the component parts that make up society operate in a way that is both functional to its members and the maintenance of society as a whole.

1 With which of the 'founders' of sociology is functionalism most closely associated? `1 mark`

....

2 What is meant by social order? `2 marks`

....

....

3 What did Talcott Parsons mean when he referred to society as a social system? `2 marks`

....

....

4 Explain what functionalists mean by the principle of meritocracy. `3 marks`

....

....

....

5 What do functionalists mean by functional prerequisites? `3 marks`

....

....

....

6 How do functionalists believe social order is maintained? `4 marks`

....

....

....

....

....

Marxism

Marxism is a structural-conflict theory based on the class conflict that stems from people's relationship to the means of production. Compared to functionalism, Marxism is much better equipped to deal with and explain social change, since this is a cornerstone of Marx's theory.

1 What do Marxists call profit derived from the exploitation of the proletariat? `1 mark`

....

2 What do Marxists mean by the means of production? `2 marks`

....

....

3 What do Marxists mean by the forces of production? `2 marks`

....

....

4 What is meant by the infrastructure? `3 marks`

....

....

....

5 What is meant by the superstructure? `3 marks`

....

....

....

6 In what ways do Marxists see 'bourgeois (ruling class) ideology' as important? `4 marks`

....

....

....

....

....

Interactionism

As a perspective interactionism is fundamentally different to both functionalism and Marxism. It rejects any attempt to make sense of society as a system, choosing instead to try to understand the meanings behind individual actions.

1 What terms do interactionists use to refer to what people see themselves as? `1 mark`

....

2 What is meant by the term 'master status'? `1 mark`

....

....

3 What is meant by free will? `2 marks`

....

....

4 What do interactionists mean by the idea of negotiation? `2 marks`

....

....

....

5 What is meant by the process of labelling? `3 marks`

....

....

....

6 What is meant by the process of self-fulfilling prophecy? `4 marks`

....

....

....

....

....

Feminism

The starting point for feminism is to highlight the generally unequal situation and experiences of women compared to men. It is a perspective by women for women that is political in that it actively seeks to produce a better world for women.

1 What *two* significant pieces of legislation introduced in the 1970s helped move gender equality forwards? `2 marks`

a

....

b

....

2 What is meant by patriarchy? `1 mark`

....

....

3 Give *two* examples, highlighted by Marxist-feminists, whereby women's position is generally worse than men's? `2 marks`

a

....

b

....

4 How does the position of liberal feminists differ to more radical feminists? `2 marks`

....

....

5 How might the domestic position of some women in minority ethnic groups be different to women in general? `3 marks`

....

....

....

6 How might life history research offer an insight into the experiences of women? `4 marks`

....

....

....

....

....

New Right

This is sometimes called 'political functionalism' because the New Right shares so much in common with functionalism, such as support for a meritocratic society and support for the traditional family. With the decline of functionalism New Right thinkers became the new right-wing voice of sociology.

1 Which prime minister is most closely associated with introducing New Right ideas in the 1980s?   `1 mark`

....

2 What is meant by neo-liberalism (sometimes called neo-conservatism)?   `2 marks`

....

....

3 What policies have New Right thinkers advocated as a way of driving up standards in public services like education and health care?   `2 marks`

....

....

....

4 What do the New Right mean by a culture of poverty?   `3 marks`

....

....

....

5 What do the New Right mean by a culture of dependency?   `3 marks`

....

....

....

....

6 Outline Charles Murray's criticisms of the underclass.   `4 marks`

....

....

....

....

....

Exam-style questions

1 Which of the following theories could be described as a consensus theory? `1 mark`

  a   Feminism

  b   Functionalism

  c   Marxism

  d   Interactionism

2 Which of the following sociological perspectives is associated with the idea of an alienated proletariat? `1 mark`

  a   Feminism

  b   Functionalism

  c   Marxism

  d   Interactionism

3 What is meant by the Weberian concept of life chances? `3 marks`

....

....

....

....

4 Identify and describe what Durkheim meant by anomie. `3 marks`

....

....

....

....

Item A

Wilkinson and Pickett (2009) in their book *The Spirit Level* undertook statistical analysis to show that everyone in society (including, interestingly, the rich) are worse off when there is inequality in society. They argue that almost all social problems improve as society becomes more equal.

5 From Item A, examine *one* strength of using official statistics. **2 marks**

....

....

....

6 Identify and explain *one* disadvantage of using structured interviews to investigate class consciousness. **4 marks**

....

....

....

....

7 Discuss the view that society is meritocratic. **12 marks**

Use the space below to plan your answer and complete it on a separate piece of paper.

....

....

....

....

....

....

....

....

Social structures, social processes and social issues

Social structures, processes and issues

Both functionalists and Marxists are critical of interactionists for ignoring the importance and significance of social structures in having a direct impact on people's lives. Marxists argue that the structure of social class is particularly important.

1 What do sociologists understand by the term 'social structure'? `2 marks`

....

....

2 Give an example of a social structure other than social class. `1 mark`

....

3 What is a social process? `2 marks`

....

....

4 What is a social issue? `2 marks`

....

....

5 What are sanctions and how do they help reinforce behaviour? `5 marks`

....

....

....

....

....

....

Sociological debates (consensus and conflict; grand theory versus microsociology)

When the founders of sociology first applied their ideas to the real world, they were particularly trying to understand the sweeping changes that were transforming previously agricultural societies into the modern urban societies characteristic of industrial capitalism. However, over time Marxists and functionalists have developed two very different approaches to explain how societies operate.

1 What is meant by the term 'consensus'? `1 mark`

....

2 Give an example of a consensus perspective. `1 mark`

....

3 What is a conflict perspective? `2 marks`

....

4 Give an example of a conflict perspective. `1 mark`

....

5 What are new social movements? `2 marks`

....

....

....

6 Using examples, explain what is meant by the term 'grand theory'. `4 marks`

....

....

....

....

....

Culture and nature

The practice of sociology involves gaining knowledge about ourselves, the societies in which we live and the people who make up that society. It is the study of the links between people and society. It is through culture that we are able to make sense of society.

1 **What is culture?** `2 marks`

....

....

....

2 **What is meant by a subculture?** `2 marks`

....

....

....

3 **Differentiate between 'nature' and 'nurture'.** `2 marks`

....

....

....

4 **How do feral children illustrate the important process of socialisation?** `3 marks`

....

....

....

....

5 **How is social control maintained in societies?** `4 marks`

....

....

....

....

....

Sex and gender

Feminists make the point that all women suffer from male oppression and the unfair structures of patriarchy, but the individual life chances of each woman can vary enormously and are shaped particularly by the economic forces of social class.

1 Define what sociologists mean by sex.　　　　　　　　　　　　　　　　　　　　1 mark

....

....

2 Explain the meaning of gender.　　　　　　　　　　　　　　　　　　　　　　2 marks

....

....

3 Give an example (for each sex) of how culture can influence gender roles in girls and boys.　　　　　　　　　　　　　　　　　　　　　　　　　　2 marks

....

....

....

....

4 Explain what control people have over their gender identities.　　　　　　4 marks

....

....

....

....

5 What contribution has the feminist perspective made to challenging traditional gender roles for women?　　　　　　　　　　　　　　　　　　5 marks

....

....

....

....

....

....

Race and ethnicity

Bias towards different ethnic groups can lead to prejudice and discrimination. If migrants are viewed as racially or ethnically different, such as having different skin colour or accents, this can lead to prejudice and discrimination against them.

1 Differentiate between the terms 'race' and 'ethnicity'. 2 marks

....

....

....

....

2 What is racial prejudice? 2 marks

....

....

....

3 What is racial discrimination? 2 marks

....

....

....

4 Explain the term 'ethnocentrism'. 1 mark

....

....

....

5 In what ways can racial prejudice be linked to the historical practice of colonialism? 4 marks

....

....

....

....

....

....

....

Facts and values

The methodological approach of positivism, so favoured by Emile Durkheim, argues that the only source of objective knowledge is through the scientific method. It maintains that the study of society should centre around facts, which must be subject to observation.

1 What is a sociological fact? `1 mark`

....

....

2 What are values? `2 marks`

....

....

....

3 Briefly outline the functionalist position with regard to values, both in terms of making society function and how values are viewed when undertaking research. `4 marks`

....

....

....

....

....

4 How is an interactionist's approach to research different from a functionalist in terms of values? `3 marks`

....

....

....

....

....

5 How does agency differ from structure in terms of explaining people's behaviour? `4 marks`

....

....

....

....

....

Exam-style questions

1 Which of the following is an example of agency behaviour? `1 mark`

   a   Schools imposing compulsory revision sessions.

   b   Schools giving out a detention.

   c   An individual choosing to truant.

   d   School fees restricting recruitment to poorer children.

....

2 Which of the following statements does not support the view that sociological research should be scientific? `1 mark`

   a   All evidence collected should be empirical.

   b   The sole purpose of sociology should be the collection of facts.

   c   All research should aim to be objective.

   d   Sociologists should subjectively interpret the meanings behind people's behaviour.

....

3 Identify and describe *one* example of what is meant by a conflict perspective. `3 marks`

....

....

....

....

....

4 Describe what is meant by the marketisation of education. `3 marks`

....

....

....

....

....

....

....

Item A

Focus groups can be useful in making sense of the processes and practices that people can use in their attempt to put some sense of order into their lives. The line between the public and the private is not always a clear one – it is a boundary that shifts and one that can vary across cultures and time. Culture is central to our lives and to who we are.

Adapted from Blakeley, G. (2014) 'Ordering Lives' in Allen, J. and Blakeley, G. (eds.) *Understanding Social Lives, Part 1,* Milton Keynes: The Open University.

5 From Item A, examine *one* weakness of using focus groups or group interviews. **2 marks**

....

....

....

....

6 Identify and explain *one* advantage of using unstructured interviews of a one-to-one nature when researching people's private lives. **4 marks**

....

....

....

....

....

....

....

7 Discuss what is meant by the statement 'Culture is central to our lives and to who we are.' **12 marks**

Use the space below to plan your answer and complete it on a separate piece of paper.

....

....

....

....

....

....

....

Research

The scientific method (quantitative research)

When sociologists collect their own data, this is known as primary data. In contemporary society the quantitative approach is used when researchers want to obtain entire trends or statistical truths from their research. So, for example, examination data that indicates that girls do substantially better at GCSE with A*–C grades is an example of quantitative data.

1 Briefly outline what positivism is. **2 marks**

....

....

2 What is meant by quantitative data? **1 mark**

....

....

3 Which *two* research methods are most commonly associated with quantitative research? **2 marks**

a
....

b
....

4 Explain the meaning of the terms 'reliability' and 'validity'. **4 marks**

Reliability is: ....

....

....

Validity is: ....

....

....

5 Outline *three* advantages of using quantitative research. **6 marks**

a
....

....

b
....

....

c
....

....

Interpretive methods (qualitative research)

Those who gather and use qualitative data are known collectively as interpretivist sociologists because they try to interpret the motives and meanings that lie behind people's actions. It is modelled on Max Weber's approach, which he called 'verstehen'.

1. What does it mean when research is described as subjective? `2 marks`

....

....

2. What is qualitative research? `3 marks`

....

....

....

3. Identify *two* primary research methods commonly used in qualitative research. `2 marks`

a ....

b ....

4. Why is the qualitative approach described as subjective rather than objective? `3 marks`

....

....

....

....

5. Explain why qualitative data is generally viewed as rich in validity. `4 marks`

....

....

....

....

....

....

Primary and secondary sources

When sociologists collect their own data, this is known as primary data. It has the advantage of researchers being in control of how the data was collected and they can ensure the source of the data is trustworthy.

1 What are primary sources?   `2 marks`

....

....

2 What is a sample?   `2 marks`

....

....

....

3 What is meant by secondary data?   `2 marks`

....

....

....

....

4 Give *one* example of a quantitative secondary source and one example of
a qualitative secondary source.   `2 marks`

Quantitative source: ....

....

Qualitative source: ....

....

....

5 Why is there a need for some secondary sources to be used with caution?   `4 marks`

....

....

....

....

....

....

Surveys and questionnaires

Self-completion questionnaires involve respondents answering questions in their own words. This research method is most associated with the approach of positivism and is generally used to collect quantitative data in response to closed questions.

1 What alternative medium could be used for questionnaires besides paper? `1 mark`

....

....

2 What is a closed question? `2 marks`

....

....

....

3 Explain why questionnaires are not very good at collecting qualitative data. `3 marks`

....

....

....

....

4 Outline briefly why questionnaires tend to produce data higher in reliability. `3 marks`

....

....

....

....

5 Explain how having the potential to have larger sample sizes is an advantage associated with using questionnaires. `4 marks`

....

....

....

....

....

Interviews

Research obtained from focus groups has been given to the general synod of the Church of England, which as an organisation has followed the example of the political parties by resorting to focus groups to tell it what it is doing wrong. The findings were that young people saw it as an isolated club, constantly tearing itself apart and trying vainly to be trendy.

1 What type of data is likely to be collected using structured interviews?   `1 mark`

....

2 Explain what a focus group is.   `2 marks`

....

....

....

3 Outline *two* advantages of using semi-structured interviews compared to structured interviews.   `4 marks`

a ....

....

b ....

....

4 Why do unstructured interviews produce rich qualitative data, high in validity?   `3 marks`

....

....

....

....

5 What is meant by the interviewer effect?   `4 marks`

....

....

....

....

....

....

Observation

Observation can take the form of being either participant or non-participant. As a research method it is associated with qualitative data and the generation of data high in validity.

1 What does it mean when observation is covert? `1 mark`

....

....

2 What is meant by an observation schedule? `2 marks`

....

....

....

3 What is non-participant observation? `3 marks`

....

....

....

....

4 Explain what the observer effect is. `3 marks`

....

....

....

....

5 What is the purpose of an observation schedule? `5 marks`

....

....

....

....

....

....

....

Statistics

Positivists argue that the collection of quantitative data in the form of statistics reflects a rigorous methodological approach based on the collection of objective evidence in the form of facts. However, interpretive sociologists argue statistical data needs to be treated with caution.

1 What are official statistics?   `1 mark`

....

....

2 Explain what nominal data is.   `2 marks`

....

....

....

3 Explain the difference between the mean and mode averages.   `4 marks`

Mean: ....

....

Mode: ....

....

4 With regard to the Item above, why do interpretive sociologists say that statistical data needs to be treated with caution?   `3 marks`

....

....

....

....

5 Briefly explain the process of converting raw data into a report of findings.   `4 marks`

....

....

....

....

....

....

Exam-style questions

1 Which of the following would be most appropriate for the collection of quantitative data? `1 mark`

a Participant observation

b Unstructured interviews

c Questionnaires

d Focus groups

....

2 Which of the following would be most associated with reliability? `1 mark`

a Unstructured interviews

b Semi-structured interviews

c Questionnaires

d Focus groups

....

3 Describe what is meant by peer review in research. `3 marks`

....

....

....

....

....

....

....

4 Describe the meaning of valid data. `3 marks`

....

....

....

....

....

....

....

....

Item A

Natalie Jolly undertook an overt observation of the Amish, a religious sect who reject most aspects of modern American society. She gained access to this community through working as a midwife's assistant. Jolly describes the tension she felt between becoming a fully active participant and a completely detached passive spectator.

Adapted from: Jolly, N. (2014) 'In this world but not of it: Midwives, Amish, and the politics of power'. *Sociological Research Online*, 19 (2), 13.

5 **From Item A, examine *one* weakness of using overt observation.**

2 marks

....

....

....

....

6 **Identify and explain *one* advantage of using observation when studying groups like the Amish.**

4 marks

....

....

....

....

....

....

7 **Discuss when and why researchers might use a pilot study.**

12 marks

Use the space below to plan your answer and complete it on a separate piece of paper.

....

....

....

....

....

....

....

....

....

....

....

Families

What is a family?

Defining the family is a complex and contested task. Changes to the family means that it has become diverse with the traditional nuclear family no longer necessarily considered as the 'norm'. Changes to the family inevitably affect contemporary definitions.

1 Define the term 'nuclear family'. `1 mark`

....

....

2 Explain what is meant by the extended family. `2 marks`

....

....

3 Explain why people may live in a single-person household. `3 marks`

....

....

....

....

....

4 Using the idea of the family life cycle, discuss why sociologists like Robert Chester still see the nuclear family as important. `3 marks`

....

....

....

....

5 How have changes in the law affected the family? `4 marks`

....

....

....

....

....

Conjugal role relationships

One of the greatest social changes across Europe in recent decades has been the increase of women in the labour market. Dual earner-based partnerships are becoming normal. However, changes in women's work patterns have not always been matched by changes in the division of conjugal roles.

1 What is meant by the term 'conjugal role'? `1 mark`

....

....

2 What do functionalist sociologists say about conjugal roles? `2 marks`

....

....

....

3 What is meant by Young and Willmott's term 'symmetrical family'? `3 marks`

....

....

....

....

4 What is meant by the 'dual burden' or 'double shift' when applied to women? `3 marks`

....

....

....

....

5 What is the principle of stratified diffusion and what predictions did Young and Willmott make about the family in the future? `4 marks`

....

....

....

....

....

....

Alternatives to the family

In her novel *Woman on the Edge of Time*, Marge Piercy imagines a world where children are raised by groups of three male or female 'co-mothers'. Other novelists, such as Toni Morrison have challenged the wisdom of the traditional nuclear family, arguing that children would be better raised by a whole community.

1 What proportion of households contain only one person? `1 mark`

....

....

2 Give *two* examples of why young people may not live in a conventional family. `2 marks`

a ....

....

b ....

....

3 Why do you think there are nearly twice as many men as women aged 25–44 living alone? `3 marks`

....

....

....

....

4 What is communal living? `3 marks`

....

....

....

....

5 Explain why house share has risen for adults. `4 marks`

....

....

....

....

....

....

Family functions

In 2017, a photographic exhibition was opened in London's National Portrait Gallery called 'We Are Family'. Its aim was to show the importance that shared mealtimes serve in promoting positive experiences and outcomes for family members. Research published in 2015 showed that an increasing number of parents are making an effort to change from eating in front of the television in favour of the perceived benefits of sitting together, enjoying a meal as a family around the table.

1. What are Murdock's *four* universal functions of the family?   4 marks

   a ....

   ....

   b ....

   ....

   c ....

   ....

   d ....

   ....

2. What are the *two* 'basic and irreducible' family functions according to Parsons?   2 marks

   a ....

   b ....

3. Explain what is meant when the functionalist perspective is described as 'warm bath' theory.   3 marks

   ....

   ....

   ....

   ....

4. Give *two* examples of how 'warm bath' theory can be criticised.   2 marks

   ....

   ....

   ....

5. Identify *two* sociological perspectives that would not support the 'warm bath' theory.   2 marks

   a ....

   b ....

6. Using the Item above, discuss some of the positive functions a family might derive from eating together.   4 marks

   ....

   ....

   ....

   ....

Changes in family structure over time

In her book *All Must Have Prizes* Melanie Phillips argues that the culture of disciplined parenting is breaking down due to liberal ideas that children have rights and the increasing role of the media and peer groups in shaping a child's identity than parents.

1 According to Talcott Parsons, what was the typical structure of the pre-industrial family?

1 mark

....

....

2 In what way does the research of Peter Laslett challenge Parsons?

2 marks

....

....

....

3 Explain why the nuclear family encouraged mobility during industrialisation.

3 marks

....

....

....

....

4 Briefly outline *three* key characteristics of contemporary families.

3 marks

a
....

b
....

c
....

5 Explain how the relationship between children and parents has changed from pre-industrial times.

5 marks

....

....

....

....

....

....

....

Marriage and divorce

In 2017 the government announced that all married couples will now be able to apply for a divorce online using a 'smart form', with questions based on the circumstances of the marriage breakdown. A spokeswoman for HM Courts and Tribunals Service said for divorcing couples it will lead to a reduction in paperwork and processing time.

1 What does polygamy mean?   `1 mark`

....

....

2 Explain the meaning of serial monogamy.   `2 marks`

....

....

....

3 What has happened to the marriage rate in the past 60 years?   `2 marks`

....

....

....

4 Why did the Divorce Reform Act (1969) have such a significant impact?   `3 marks`

....

....

....

....

5 Briefly compare and contrast functionalist with feminist explanations of divorce.   `4 marks`

....

....

....

....

....

....

Exam-style questions

1 Which sociologist claimed that some form of the nuclear family existed in every one of the 250 societies that he studied, making it 'universal'?   `1 mark`

  a   Talcott Parsons

  b   Edmund Leach

  c   George Murdock

  d   William Goode

....

2 Which of the following terms did Parsons use to describe the role of women as biologically suited to the emotional and cultural role of domesticity?   `1 mark`

  a   Instrumental

  b   Economic

  c   Conjugal

  d   Expressive

....

3 Describe what Leach meant by the term 'cereal packet image of the family'.   `3 marks`

....

....

....

....

....

....

4 Identify and describe *one* type of family diversity recognised by Rapoport and Rapoport.   `3 marks`

....

....

....

....

....

....

....

Item A

Heath, McGhee and Trevena (2011) undertook research into household and family formation among recent migrants from Poland, who had been resident in Britain for at least 12 months. Their research approach consisted of in-depth interviews with 20 migrants in four locations. They found a mundane 'ordinariness' of many aspects of migrants' family lives. At the same time, they found that making and reinforcing connections with extended kin in Poland was an important characteristic of their sample of families.

5 From Item A, examine *one* weakness of using in-depth interviews. `2 marks`

....

....

6 Identify and explain *one* advantage of using self-complete questionnaires to investigate the division of labour within families. `4 marks`

....

....

....

....

....

....

7 Discuss how far sociologists agree that the nuclear family is still important in modern British society. `12 marks`

Use the space below to plan your answer and complete it on a separate piece of paper.

....

....

....

....

....

....

....

....

....

....

Education

Roles and functions of education

William Forster's Elementary Education Act had the effect of introducing compulsory state education to England and Wales. However, prior to this it is estimated that as many as 95 per cent of children of elementary school age were already receiving some form of school education.

1 Explain the term 'compulsory state education'. `1 mark`

2 Explain what is meant by the hidden curriculum. `2 marks`

3 In what ways do functionalists argue education promotes social cohesion? `3 marks`

4 Explain Durkheim's view that education creates an important division of labour. `3 marks`

5 Briefly outline the functionalist case that education promotes a meritocracy. `4 marks`

The relationship between education and capitalism

Marxists see the education system as supporting capitalism by ensuring that working-class students are prepared for mundane repetitive labour, while middle-class students are encouraged to use schooling as a way of making connections and getting on in life.

1 **What is capitalism?** `1 mark`

....

....

2 **How would Marxists see the role of socialisation in education?** `2 marks`

....

....

....

3 **What did Bowles and Gintis mean by the 'correspondence principle'?** `3 marks`

....

....

....

4 **How does the work of Paul Willis challenge correspondence theory?** `3 marks`

....

....

....

5 **Briefly outline *three* criticisms of the Marxist perspective on education.** `6 marks`

a ....

....

b ....

....

c ....

....

Educational achievement (social class)

Although only 7 per cent of the population attend private schools, they account for 71 per cent of senior judges, 62 per cent of senior armed forces officers, 55 per cent of senior civil servants, 53 per cent of senior diplomats and 50 per cent of members of the House of Lords.

(Adapted from: *Elitist Britain* (2014) published by Social Mobility and Child Poverty Commission)

1 **What is meant by the term 'cultural capital' in the context of education?**   `1 mark`

....

....

2 **What is the link between social class and educational achievement?**   `2 marks`

....

....

....

3 **Why do sociologists use free school meals as an important measure of social class attainment?**   `3 marks`

....

....

....

....

4 **What is the purpose of the 'pupil premium'?**   `3 marks`

....

....

....

....

5 **In what ways did Kerris Cooper and Kitty Stewart find that material deprivation served to undermine children's educational achievements?**   `4 marks`

....

....

....

....

....

....

Educational achievement (gender)

Since the 1980s there have been a number of policies designed to encourage girls into science and technology. These include GIST (Girls into Science and Technology) and WISE (Women into Science and Engineering).

1 What has happened to attainment levels of boys in the past 30 years? `1 mark`

....

....

2 At what levels do females outperform males in the education system? `2 marks`

....

....

....

3 Explain how the Education Reform Act (1988) is seen to have helped girls. `3 marks`

....

....

....

....

....

4 Are there gender patterns of subject choice? `3 marks`

....

....

....

....

....

5 Briefly outline the contribution of feminism to improved female attainment. `4 marks`

....

....

....

....

....

....

....

Educational achievement ('race' and ethnicity)

Education

According to the DfE, in 2017 around a third of all pupils in the education system are ethnic minorities. Attainment statistics show some ethnic groups do better than average, while other ethnic groups underachieve compared to the white majority.

1 Which is the best performing ethnic group in education? `1 mark`

....

2 What is exclusion and which ethnic group is most likely to be excluded? `2 marks`

....

....

....

3 Which minority ethnic groups are more likely to experience material deprivation and how might this impact upon education? `3 marks`

....

....

....

....

....

4 How might cultural capital be seen to play a role in educational success among some minority ethnic groups? `3 marks`

....

....

....

....

....

5 Briefly explain how social class and gender also impact upon ethnic group patterns of educational achievement. `5 marks`

....

....

....

....

....

....

....

43

Educational policies

There have been many significant changes to education through educational policies. State education, and the policies that have shaped it, have invariably had a political dimension to them, reflecting the ideas of the political party in power at the time.

1 What was the tripartite system? `1 mark`

....

....

2 What type of school was introduced in 1965? `1 mark`

....

3 What are free schools? `2 marks`

....

....

4 Why do schools lead to inequalities in education because of catchment area? `3 marks`

....

....

5 What is meant by the marketisation of education? `3 marks`

....

....

....

....

6 How have government policies transformed higher education? `4 marks`

....

....

....

....

....

....

Exam-style questions

1 Which sociologist is associated with the term 'cultural capital'? `1 mark`

a Talcott Parsons

b Pierre Bourdieu

c Stephen Ball

d Halsey, Heath and Ridge

....

2 Which of the following sociological perspectives would support the idea that we live in a meritocracy? `1 mark`

a Functionalism

b Marxism

c Feminism

d Interactionism

....

3 Describe what faith schools are. `3 marks`

....

....

....

....

....

4 Describe and identify *one* criticism of setting and streaming. `3 marks`

....

....

....

....

....

....

Item A

Research using questionnaires by Durham University (2016) has found that pupils who attend private schools benefit from an equivalent to two years of extra schooling over state school pupils, even after adjusting for social and economic bias. This suggests that the benefits in terms of attainment from going to a private school are larger than previously thought.

5 From Item A, examine *one* weakness of using questionnaires. `2 marks`

....

....

....

....

6 Identify and explain *one* advantage of using participant observation to classroom interaction. `4 marks`

....

....

....

....

....

7 Discuss the view that working class underachievement in education is caused by factors outside school. `12 marks`

Use the space below to plan your answer and then complete it.

....

....

....

....

....

....

....

....

....

....

....

....

The Publishers would like to thank the following for permission to reproduce copyright material.

Acknowledgements

Every effort has been made to trace all copyright holders, but if any have been inadvertently overlooked, the Publishers will be pleased to make the necessary arrangements at the first opportunity.

Although every effort has been made to ensure that website addresses are correct at time of going to press, Hodder Education cannot be held responsible for the content of any website mentioned in this book. It is sometimes possible to find a relocated web page by typing in the address of the home page for a website in the URL window of your browser.

Hachette UK's policy is to use papers that are natural, renewable and recyclable products and made from wood grown in sustainable forests. The logging and manufacturing processes are expected to conform to the environmental regulations of the country of origin.

Orders: please contact Bookpoint Ltd, 130 Park Drive, Milton Park, Abingdon, Oxon OX14 4SE. Fax: (44) 01235 400401.
Email education@bookpoint.co.uk Lines are open from 9 a.m. to 5 p.m., Monday to Saturday, with a 24-hour message answering service. You can also order through our website: www.hoddereducation.co.uk

ISBN: 978 1 5104 3518 6

First published in 2018 by
Hodder Education,
An Hachette UK Company
Carmelite House
50 Victoria Embankment
London EC4Y 0DZ

www.hoddereducation.co.uk

Impression number 10 9 8 7 6 5 4 3 2 1

Year   2022 2021 2020 2019 2018

Cover photo © Natalia Sheinkin/Shutterstock.com

Typeset by Integra Software Services Pvt. Ltd, Pondicherry, India

Printed and bound in Spain

A catalogue record for this title is available from the British Library.

HODDEREDUCATION

t: 01235 827827

e: education@bookpoint.co.uk

w: hoddereducation.co.uk

ISBN 978-1-5104-3518-6

9 781510 435186

FSC
www.fsc.org

MIX
Paper from
responsible sources
FSC™ C104740